Make A

From Being Successful

to Being Significant!

by

Ron Finklestein

and

Michael LaRocca

LEADERS IN GLOBAL PUBLISHING

Other books available by the authors

The Platinum Rule for Small Business Mastery

Celebrating Success!
Fourteen Ways to Create a Successful Company

Nine Principles for Inspired Action:
A New & Targeted Perspective

49 Marketing Secrets (THAT WORK)
to Grow Sales

The Definitive Sales Handbook
How to Grow Sales and Create Lifetime Customers

Teach Yourself Creative Writing

Who Moved My Rice?

Published by Motivational Press, Inc.
2360 Corporate Circle
Suite 400
Henderson, NV 89074
www.MotivationalPress.com

www.ronfinklestein.com
MichaelEdits.com
MichaelWrites.com

Manufactured in the United States of America.

ISBN: 978-1-62865-017-4

Ron's Dedication:

To Rubin Wald who inspired this book. To Don Osborne who started me down this path. To Michael LaRocca, my coauthor, who did a great job on the book and all 1000 business owners who shared with me the secrets to their success.

Michael's Dedication:

To all the authors whose work I've edited over the years. You've taught me much more than you know.

Contents

Chapter One

Bob's Drive

"Why am I the only person in this office who can do sales?"

Bob is seated in an elegant office, in a luxurious black leather chair at a cherry wood desk, none of which he ever seems to notice. He's wearing a tailored gray business suit. His jacket is draped over the back of his chair.

Bob is facing Richard, who wears a tailored navy Armani suit despite holding the title Inside Sales Manager and thus rarely leaves the office. Richard begins to formulate a reply, but Bob cuts him off.

"No, scratch that," says Bob. "Okay, fine, maybe I'm not the only person who *can* do sales. But I am the only person who *will* do sales, who *does* do sales. It's not difficult. Everyone we contact needs this service. It's a great service. It's simple to see this. It's simple to explain this. But why am I the only person who's actually doing the work?"

"I –"

"Don't answer that. I'm not in the mood right now."

Bob realizes that right now's not the time for a reasoned conversation. After a brief, almost guilty look at Richard, Bob says, "Let me go calm down first. Then tell me what happened with Greg and the Eastern contract."

My reaction was unreasonable, Bob realizes as he leaves his office. *But being annoyed at this problem is not.*

Bob briefly wonders how long it'll take Richard to return to his own office, and almost smiles, but his amusement quickly gives way to his annoyance.

Bob doesn't mind doing sales. He's good at it. It's not what he would have envisioned himself doing twenty years ago, but he doesn't mind sales. Or marketing. Or customer service. Or even purchasing, receivables, payables, or payroll.

Well, maybe not payroll.

No, the problem is that he is either doing or overseeing all of them, in too much detail, being pulled in 94 different directions at once. He owns a business that grossed four hundred grand last year and he's still working harder than he would in a 9-to-5.

It just doesn't make sense.

Bob enters the break room and is halfway to the water fountain before he stops. The table is cluttered with napkins and plates. On the counter beside the sink are several bottles of soda.

Unfortunately, Bob's secretary chooses just that moment to open the opposite door and enter the break room. Ella's smart "office chic" business suit, silk blouse, expensive shoes, and styled black hair make her look almost as efficient as she actually is.

"This is just ridiculous." Bob throws his hands in the air. "Am I a business owner or a babysitter?"

"Bob, I thought you were —" she begins.

"Am I the only person who is even marginally engaged in this place? I can't believe I have to tell you to keep the kitchen area clean, to take out the trash, to answer the customer emails on the same day. It's ridiculous that you don't know all this. It's ridiculous that you aren't already doing all this. Is it ignorance or apathy? No, wait, let me guess — you don't know and you don't care."

Ella knows this isn't true. She also knows that Bob knows this isn't true. She enjoys working for him most of the time, but he can overreact on occasion. She suspects it's the result of keeping such a tight lid on his feelings, but it wouldn't be appropriate to tell him that.

The atypical situation in the break room leaves Ella

stunned for a moment. In that moment, Bob leaves the room. He's out of the building before she ever gets the chance to tell him that the so-called mess was in fact Bob's workers setting up the break room for his 45th birthday party.

Bob quickly drives his silver luxury sedan from the parking lot, enjoying its smooth handling and easy power. He always enjoys the first minute of every drive, before his thoughts and plans move to the front of his mind and distract him from his surroundings. The first car he looked at cost more than he was willing to spend, but he likes what he bought instead.

He drives half a block along the access road, stops at the intersection where it meets the four-lane "proper" road, turns left when the light changes, and starts using his hands-free phone.

"Ella, it's Bob. I'm sorry about that. Really. I shouldn't have done that, okay?"

"Sure."

"I'm going to Eastern to see if I can save this contract. I don't know when I'll be back. I'll keep you posted."

"Okay."

Bob drives his car onto the interstate and accelerates rapidly. He notices that Ella seems subdued, which makes him feel guilty. "I'm sorry I blew up back there. You do a great job. I'd be lost without you."

"No problem."

"Okay. Bye."

Bob ends the call, swerves around someone who apparently doesn't realize that interstates also have minimum speed limits, and makes another call.

"I'm sorry I blew up back there," he tells Richard's voicemail. "It's not your fault. Since this is a local customer for a change, I'm going down there to save this one in person. Keep pulling those numbers together. I'll catch up with you later."

After quickly checking his GPS to remind himself which exit to take, confirming that his memory is accurate, he makes another call.

"Greg," he says. "Bob. Tell me what happened."

"I —"

"Give me the short version."

Greg pauses. "The guy with the title Purchasing Manager does not, in fact, make purchasing decisions."

Bob exhales.

"Exactly," says Greg. "All that effort explaining what we do, winning over a guy – and we did win him over – who can't say yes or no. He's got to go run it by his boss, and we've never spoken to her at all –"

"And he'll lose something in translation."

"Right," says Greg. "That's exactly right."

"So we find out who she is and then we start over again." Bob bangs on his steering wheel in frustration.

"It gets worse. While we were busy with the gatekeeper, Dickson got to the company president. She's the one making the decisions."

"Oh… fudge." Bob breathes deeply. "Dickson. How did they find out who the decision maker is before we –? No, never mind how they found out. The question is, how do we fix this?"

Oh great, he thinks, flipping on his headlights and windshield wipers. *Rain.*

"Recommendations," says Greg. "Testimonials."

"What about them?"

"If we start over now, we sound like salesmen."

"That could be because we are salesman," says Bob, chuckling.

"We know why we're different from our competition, why Eastern should hire us instead. But we can talk ourselves blue in the face explaining that and it won't be as effective as recommendations from our customers."

"This is true," says Bob. "But unless you know how to get our customers to drop whatever they're doing and just jump in ahead of Dickson right now to tell Eastern just how great we are…"

Ahead of Bob, a car brakes suddenly. The lanes on this stretch of interstate have a way of suddenly ending or turning exit-only and panicking those unfamiliar with it, so he isn't surprised, but he is annoyed. He swerves left and wonders why he's so easily annoyed these days.

"We could always sabotage them," Greg mutters, followed by a noise that doesn't travel well from hands-free phone to hands-free phone.

"Did you just laugh nervously?" Bob asks.

"What?"

"I've read about that in books – oh, how I wish I had

time to read books again – but I don't believe I've ever heard it before. Was that a nervous laugh?"

"Um… no… um, I was just joking about sabotage –"

"Of course you were joking. Sabotage would be unethical."

"It would," Greg quickly agrees.

"So we don't do that. We don't sabotage Dickson. We reframe the job."

"Reframe."

"Sure. Reframe. If we're bidding against an incumbent, we make the old entrenched methods look bad. If we're the incumbent, we make our insider knowledge critical. If we've got a better reputation for data security, we play up the threat and likelihood of compromising a system. If none of our competitors provide a single point of contact, stress that we do and why it matters. If we've got a less experienced team, we play down the need for expertise and talk up our ability to do the same work at lower cost. If we've got a more experienced team, we play up the value of experience, and the peace of mind they'll enjoy knowing that our people are all hired, trained, and in place. Make what we do best seem vital and what others do well seem not so important. Stress the critical importance of anything we know that our competitor doesn't. Reframe."

"Ah," says Greg.

"Ideally before they call for bids, of course." Bob takes the exit that leads from the interstate he's on to the interstate he wants to be on. "Oh, have they called for bids on this yet?"

"Not yet."

"Great! We are in there! We can help them decide what to stress in the RFP. If Dickson can beat us on what *does* matter to the customer, we bid on what *should* matter to the customer. Can you meet me in –"

Bob is driving in the leftmost of five lanes, which quickly narrow to four and then three lanes, and he needs to shoot to the far right lane within the next mile. This particular stretch of interstate brings out the worst in the lane jockeys, no matter the weather, especially if there's a slow-moving bus or truck.

Bob is momentarily distracted by his phone call and therefore unaware of the car on his right, in his blind spot.

The car veers to its left and smashes into Bob's car at 73 miles per hour.

The road is newly wet, when the asphalt is at its slickest. Bob's car skids. Badly.

2

Chapter Two

Law #1: The Law of Enlightened Self-Interest

What's the difference between good selfishness and bad selfishness?

At first, Bob thinks that he's sitting in a tunnel, watching the rain. Ahead of him, he can see his car, which is upside down in the wet grass. Squinting at it through the rain, he thinks it's smaller than it should be, but he doesn't know if the top is crushed or just smashed into the ground. Or both.

He can hear the traffic overhead. He looks around, eventually realizing that he's not in a tunnel at all. Rather, he's sitting under the interstate.

His next realization is that someone is sitting beside him.

The stranger is rather large, unusually tall and muscular, with the deep suntan of someone who works outdoors. He is bald on top with long blonde hair along the back and sides of his head. His black tank top is very wet from rain or sweat or both. He also wears black bicycle shorts and black tennis shoes.

Obviously not a businessman, Bob decides, but not a homeless person either. The clothes are too new.

Despite the darkness of the rain clouds, the stranger is wearing aviator sunglasses with reflective lenses. That, Bob decides, is just plain weird.

"Hi there," says the stranger. "You seem to be coming back to yourself. Oh." He offers his hand. "My name's Rynd."

"Bob." He shakes Rynd's hand. "What happened?"

"You've got a – well, you *had* a mighty fine car there. The airbag and the seat belt did their job."

"So how I'd get under here?"

"It is a fact that you should never move an injured person, except in a few specific conditions. One of those is that he's in a place that's unsafe. Like in an upside-down car in danger of drowning."

"You mean you pulled me out of there and over here?"

"No, you walked over here about two minutes ago. You need to get to a doctor. You might have had a concussion. No other injuries, though. It's amazing, really. That's a hell of a car you had there."

"Oh." Bob glances down at his clothes. No blood that he can see. No mud. He's soaked, but he's not shivering. He takes that to be a good sign. "Well, um, thank you."

"I called 911. And a tow truck. It's going to be slow going for both of them in this weather."

"Wow." Bob takes a deep breath, holds it, slowly lets it out.

"I just wish we had a dry blanket or something to wrap you in."

"It's okay." Bob pauses. "Rynd, I really appreciate it. Wow. I'm just stunned." He shakes his head. "Something like this really makes a person re-examine his priorities."

"The 911 dispatcher said I should keep you talking. And my own priorities include making sure you don't wreck another car."

"I didn't wreck it. Someone hit me."

"You remember. That's a good sign. But you could've driven defensively. Maybe. Why don't you tell me what happened?"

"Well," says Bob with a laugh, "it's probably more complicated than you've got time for."

Rynd looks directly into Bob's eyes for longer than should have been comfortable. Bob hopes he doesn't look as haggard as his reflection in the mirrored sunglasses.

Rynd says, "Try me."

Bob sighs. "I was distracted."

"Not texting, I hope."

"Never! I wish people wouldn't do that. No, I was talking to my sales manager. We're trying to stop a big contract from getting away from us. I was on my way to the customer's office."

"It's okay to be selfish," says Rynd.

"What?!"

"I didn't say greedy. I said selfish. You can't succeed without selfishness. Selfishness provides the desire, the drive, and the need to take action. It is the gas that starts the engine and keeps the wheels running and the wheels moving forward."

"Unlike my car."

Rynd matches Bob's grin. "Unlike your car. It did its job, though. But anyway, selfishness is fine, as long as it's the right kind of selfishness. For example, staying alive is probably selfish, but you shouldn't give that up."

"This is true."

"But you have to be enlightened about how you pursue your dreams, desires, and expectations. Otherwise you're just living in a tunnel."

Bob makes an exaggerated show of looking around. "What made you think of that analogy?"

Rynd grins. "I have no idea. But while you're obviously doing a fine job of being selfish in the narrow sense, narrow self-interest isn't enlightened self-interest. It's not self-interest at all, actually. It's living in a tunnel. Here's where you are, here's where you think you want to be, and you ignore everything that doesn't directly get you from here to there."

"Is that a bad thing?"

"You tell me. Bob, when your business grossed fifty thousand a year, you knew you'd be able to get another layer of support and quit working so hard when you started grossing a hundred thousand a year. When you reached a hundred thousand, you moved the goal to two hundred thousand. And when you reached two hundred thousand —"

"What is this? How do you know that?"

"It's a lucky guess. And right this minute I'm offering you that layer of support you think you need. Get out of the tunnel, Bob. As you travel your journey, you need to be aware of others and your surroundings. You need to accept what you can see and learn from them. This enlightened outlook is far more rewarding than living in a tunnel. More successful, too."

"Look, Rynd, I'm sure you helped me, although I don't remember it right now, so thanks for that. But…"

"When you reached two hundred thousand you wanted four hundred thousand. Now that you're making four hundred thousand, you're convinced that if you can break through to a million a year, you'll get another layer of support in the company and then you won't have to work so hard."

"Where'd you get those numbers?"

"You talk about methods and processes being able to scale up and down, but don't you see that your goals are doing the same thing? They'll just keep scaling up. You're frustrated, Bob."

"I am."

"Disillusioned, trapped, lost. You've hit a wall."

Bob follows Rynd's gaze to the remains of his car. "So you're telling me the dollar figure isn't an end, just a means to an end. I know that, Rynd."

"You know it on the surface, Bob, but you're not feeling it deep down. Look below the surface. If you do what you've always done, you'll get what you've always gotten. That, too, sounds like fortune cookie wisdom, but it's because you're only looking at the surface. Feel it in your gut."

"So you're saying I need to... to do something other than set that million dollars as a milestone. Change something."

"What you're doing now isn't working. Get at why you're doing it and see what you find."

"Be selfish."

"Be selfish. But know this. Chasing a narrow definition of what's selfish is not in your best interest. You need to get out of your tunnel and embrace an all-encompassing vision of what we should call enlightened self-interest. Be the good kind of selfish. Then you'll be truly fulfilled."

"The good kind of selfish?" Bob asks.

"The good kind of selfish. Your enlightened self-interest should include spiritual selfishness, financial self-interest, relationships, and health objectives. Define how others can help you and don't be afraid to ask for help. Ask them how you can help them. Focus on how family can contribute to your goals through support, love, and inspiration. They want you to be successful."

"I need a personal vision to live by," Bob realizes. "Everybody does, actually. Otherwise it's just doing stuff, maybe a little bit of stuff and maybe a lot of stuff, but just some random stuff. Not always the right stuff. Not always the wrong stuff either. Just random stuff."

Rynd nods. "That's right. Random stuff. I like that."

Bob looks around. He sees no rescue vehicles, nobody stopping to investigate, nothing requiring his immediate attention. He turns back to Rynd.

"Tell me more."

3

Chapter Three

Law #2: The Law of Total Ownership

How can you change what you don't own?

"You need to focus on your enlightened self-interest, Bob. That's how true greatness occurs."

"You're saying I can be great by being selfish."

"I say that being selfish is the only way you can be great. I know that flies in the face of conventional wisdom, but so what? Let it. True unselfishness comes from being completely and totally selfish."

"I'm not sure if that's a Zen koan or a tweet from a lunatic."

"Keep an open mind, Bob. Why are you doing what you're doing now? You know, living the way you are, trying to get ahead the same way that everybody else is. Because you're just doing what everybody else does, that's why. You're not owning your life. And even if you do win at this game you're playing, you won't be happy. Actually, a lot of people would say you've already won. Wouldn't they?"

"What?"

"Homeowner, no mortgage, owner of a successful business, married for twenty years, two grown children with careers of their own –"

"How do you know so much about me?"

"That is an excellent question, but is it the most important one right this minute?"

"It might be."

"Or not. You're what a lot of people would call a success and you're still not happy. Do you know why? Because what you're calling winning is just taking on somebody else's definition of success. You're measuring the wrong thing entirely. Enlightened self-interest is not necessarily about more money, fame, or national recognition."

"But that could happen, right?"

"Yes, it could happen."

"I'm glad to hear it. Who are you?"

"Selfishness is about the grandmother who starts a nonprofit to help sexually abused children. It's about the sister who starts a foundation to help others deal with breast cancer. The mother who wants to put drunk drivers away. The business owner who makes a commitment to his customers and delivers on that commitment regardless of the cost, because it's the right thing to do."

"I already do that –"

"I'm sure you do, Bob. But let me ask you a question.

Do people who do charity work derive a benefit from that? Yes they do. It makes them feel good."

Bob thinks about Rynd's words. He senses some truth there.

"If you don't own it, you can't change it," says Rynd. "What makes *you* feel good?"

Bob thinks. Rynd waits.

"Sitting here talking to you isn't making me feel good, that's for sure. I need to be –"

"Due to circumstances beyond your control, there is no way you can work right now. Not in the sense of rushing to that potential customer's office and salvaging a sale, not even getting on the phone and barking orders at your people –"

"I don't bark."

"Really?"

"Well… rarely."

"Fine. But right now we're going to take a break from all that and do some big picture thinking. If not now, when?"

"Good point."

"I thought so too. It's time to make a pit stop in the race called life to determine a destination of your choosing, your enlightened self-interest, and map out the most direct course to get there."

"And later, much later, I can wonder why it took me so long to make that pit stop."

Rynd nods. "The idea of using enlightened self-interest as a business success tool demands that we think differently about our dreams, desires, and expectations of who we are and what we can become and accomplish. This is the good kind of enlightened self-interest. By being selfish, you've created a company that solves a need in the marketplace. You help people. You do what you tell your customers you're going to do. Your reliability gives them peace of mind even before you solve their problem. You provide your people good jobs and good wages and personal satisfaction, and a good life for you and your family. Oh, wait, that's a sore spot, isn't it?"

"No. Who are you?"

"Let's talk about you first, then me. Okay? Work before pleasure. Isn't that your motto?"

Bob shakes his head knowingly.

"The best work is also pleasure," says Rynd, "so you don't have to choose one or the other, but we'll get to that later. Your family."

"I'd love to spend time with them again. I'd love to just get my life back."

"But you're putting work first because to do otherwise would be…?"

Bob laughs. "I used to say selfish."

"Selfish in the narrow sense, not the enlightened sense."

"Yeah. Like that. I like owning my business but I'm not doing what I want to do. I'm doing too much and my people aren't doing enough. How can I make it fun again? How can I spend time with Debra – my wife – maybe go away for a weekend or a week, not work all the time?"

"What does your wife think?"

"I don't know. Well, I do know she thinks I bring home too much emotional distance. But that distance is how I solve problems in the office."

"It might not be a good solution in either place. What does Debra do to fill her life with meaning?"

Bob sighs. "She gave up a promising career to raise our children. And she's glad she did. That much I know. But now that they're gone, well…"

"Where is she right now?"

"One of her fundraisers." Bob pauses. "I don't know which one. But it makes her happy."

Rynd smiles knowingly. "But it makes her happy. You hear yourself, am I right?"

"You are." Bob pauses again. "I could learn from her, couldn't I?"

"You could indeed. Learning from others is always a great thing. And they can help you find your enlightened self-interest. But first, that enlightened self-interest must be a core value for you. And for the most part it usually is, but that's been more due to gut instinct and auto-pilot than deliberately being selfish, than owning your enlightened self-interest, than planning and –"

"And this is being selfish?"

"It is. Enlightened self-interest. Do you create your own future, do you truly and totally own it, or do you just stumble into it?"

Bob grins sheepishly. "Are you asking me which one I should do or which one I actually do?"

Rynd nods. "Enlightened self-interest, this concept of

creating and living by a core value, has been lost in today's society. We're too concerned about political correctness and not offending others. We're overwhelmed by the accelerated pace of change. Because things change so fast we worry about being wrong or doing the wrong things. If your enlightened self-interest is a core value for you, you cannot be wrong. Values are a personal choice on how we choose to live our lives. Are you with me?"

"I am. No concussion getting in the way."

"You're onto me." Rynd grins. "To truly have an enlightened self-interest rather than a self-centered self-interest to create greatness, you *must* focus on the development of your own abilities, talents and core values and put them to their highest and best use. The only measurement we must use is *never* thinking that our highest and best use must be at another person's expense. The development of our own enlightened self-interest is simply to allow us to do great things when called upon and being able to do so.

"Taking inspired action to achieve great things is essential. A great thing is defined as an achievement beyond your normal achievements –"

"For others," says Bob.

"That's right. For others. The great thing must be an achievement that is win-win for everyone involved. One primary test for achieving great things through the use of our enlightened self-interest is one of honesty."

"So you mean that pursuing my highest ideals is enlightened self-interest?"

"It is indeed. Being a success is about creative and intelligent people taking healthy, calculated risks to achieve their enlightened self-interest and accomplish great things. Each person is entitled to experience both the pain and benefits of the decisions they make. I believe that we are designed, from the time we are born, to actively create, grow and achieve. Starting a business is just one aspect of personal and business growth.

"If you didn't own a business, you could still express this same enlightened self-interest in your chosen profession by being the best mother or father you could be, the best pastor, health care professional, nurse or waitress you could be. Outside your business, you can express it by being the best friend, husband or parent you can be."

"I'll be glad when some health care professionals get here."

"Me too. Build your enlightened self-interest on a vision of what you want to achieve. Invest your company, profession or hobby with clarity of purpose. Build your enlightened self-interest to last not only for your lifetime but the lifetimes of your children and their children. And if you feel you've been a less than ideal parent or husband or friend or employer, own that now, and do a better job in the future."

"And it's as simple as that?" Bob asks.

"It's as simple as that. Simply put, you must own the whole of your circumstances. This means you are 100% responsible for everything that happens in your life, even if you cannot explain it. Ownership does not mean things will suddenly get easier. It simply means you can do something about the situation. The fact that you can do something is very empowering."

"But only if I do it."

Rynd smiles. "But only if you do it."

4

Chapter Four

Law #3: The Law of

Measurable Results

If we can't measure it, how do we know if it's working?

"You do a lot of things," says Rynd. "A lot of them."

"You're about to make a point."

"I am. Are you doing the right things?"

"That sounds like a loaded question."

"That could be because it is, Bob. Efficiency is doing things right, but effectiveness is doing the right things."

"But if I'm clear on what's really in my best interest," Bob realizes, "on what's truly my enlightened self-interest, then I can define the actions that achieve those goals."

"You've got it."

"Then I have to hold myself accountable – or find someone to do it for me – to achieving those goals, that enlightened self-interest."

"Exactly."

"If I own my life, and own my goals, and choose my goals based on that, and am able to measure my goals, then I can – wow. I can do a lot of things that I haven't been doing thus far, can't I?"

Rynd nods. "You can. You will."

"And my wife can help. Probably not so much with the business questions – not her specialty or her interest – but moral support, certainly. I think she'd like that. No, actually, I know she would. She's accused me of being distant, but somehow I didn't hear her."

"Maybe you were too distant."

"Real funny. And for the rest, there are co-workers, customers, colleagues, maybe even competitors. If it doesn't hurt them."

"Or a mastermind group."

"I've heard of those."

"Learn about them, Bob. They're invaluable."

"Yeah. I will."

"Bob, let's say that you know you can close one sale if you make fifty calls."

"Just for the sake of illustration, since I don't do cold calls."

"Nor should you. I never buy from someone after he's pissed me off. But these aren't cold calls. These are lukewarm sales leads, maybe from a trade show or something, and closing one sale for every fifty of these calls are numbers you've measured in your experience."

"One sale per fifty calls? Something's wrong here."

"I'm trying not to be overly optimistic. Humor me."

"Fine," Bob agrees. "Go ahead."

"When I make my fifty calls, I get ten appointments. From the ten appointments, I make one sale. This is a measurable, repeatable and predictable process. I know that if I make fifty calls and don't get ten appointments, then I need to change my approach to getting appointments. If I'm getting my ten appointments but not making my one sale, I know I need to change how I close."

"That part's realistic," Bob agrees.

"So once I figure out how to make my fifty calls, get my ten appointments and make one sale, I do the same thing over and over and over again. What I've done is to create a habit that's measurable, repeatable and predictable. As a business owner I can now train all my new sales representatives on this process. The new sales representative can now achieve the same predictable results. And if I'm not mistaken, your sales reps aren't achieving your numbers and it's causing you a bit of stress."

"You think I should train them better?"

Rynd grins. "I'm not psychic, Bob. Examine everything,

and measure everything instead of just complaining about it."

"You're blunt."

"I know. It's one of my better qualities."

Bob grins. "Great, fine, we've got a measurable process here. I can do things in my business this way. But it won't work in my personal life."

"Are you sure it won't?"

"What, are you sure it'll work at home too?"

"Hypothetically, if you were in a personal relationship – family or friend – and you were always fighting, that's a measurable result, the fighting."

"Put it in a spreadsheet?"

"Work with me, Bob." Rynd, like Bob, was grinning. "You've got a measurable result, the fighting. You can define the outcome you want, your enlightened self-interest, a reduction in the number of fights. As you try different solutions, you measure the change in the relationship by the reduction in the number of fights."

"Or increase if your solutions are really bad."

"You've got it. By taking ownership of the situation, you're empowered to change how you respond to that person you care about. By choosing to respond differently, you can expect different results. Didn't you just create a measurable, repeatable and predictable process? When you get the results you want, you can choose to implement those actions regularly."

"Hmm. That's an unusual way to express interpersonal relationships, but it makes sense. I'll buy into that."

"Or to take another example, you admitted that you bark orders at your people but only rarely."

"You want me to measure how often."

"If you don't own it, you can't change it. And if you can't measure it, you can't change it. This one's easy to measure, so do it. And remember, your personal performance is based on habits you build over a lifetime of learning. It took time to build the existing habits that you are using today. Know that when you change them, it will take some time. It takes a mental effort not to follow your usual routine. Studies have shown that when you're tired or your self-control is low, you're actually more likely to follow your habits."

"I didn't know that." Bob thinks a moment. "It makes sense though, doesn't it?"

"It does. So when you set out to change your habits, give yourself time and keep practicing the new behaviors. Be persistent. And measure what you're doing. The result will come."

"I believe it," Bob realizes. "I really do. Hey, this has been great. What about a goal of finding out who you are, getting another car, and getting back out on the road?"

Rynd laughs. "Good goals are time-bound, specific, measurable, achievable, and realistic. That's the only way they can work for you, and the only way they can be incorporated into a business so others can take the same actions."

Bob nods. "It's certainly been my experience that what I can measure is what gets my attention. My goal before I met you was time-bound, specific, and measurable. By the end of this year, I wanted to be grossing a million. Achievable and realistic… I'd sure like to think so."

"I want to look at realistic first. A billion is not, half a million probably is, a million might be. It's okay to aim a little high, okay to fail as long as you fail forward and learn from it, so I'll give you realistic. But achievable is something different."

"How?"

"Is it something you can and want to achieve? Do you really want that million, or do you want to work less and enjoy life more and do what you love? We both know you want the latter."

"But how do I measure that?"

"Measure the working hours. Measure the time you spend doing each task at your company, how much sales versus how much consulting versus how much payroll. No hours cold calling because that's never worked. Break a big vague goal like *work less and enjoy life more* into actionable, measurable steps. Otherwise you're not going to achieve much, if anything, and you won't know what is and isn't realistic."

Bob is nodding as he listens. "I see. Back when I was jogging that certainly worked. It's easy to measure times and distances, and keep raising the goals."

"Or taking swings off a golf score."

"Who told you that Debra and I like to golf?"

"Debra, I didn't know. You, it was just another lucky guess. For me, bicycling the Appalachian Trail is achievable.

For you, it could be realistic if we devised a training program with gradually increasing milestones, but it's not achievable because you just plain don't want that."

"I don't. It'd take years away from my family and my business and I wouldn't enjoy one minute of it."

"You listed family first. That's progress, Bob."

"Of course I listed them first."

"But you often put them last."

"What?!"

"You are not achieving your goals because you aren't taking the necessary action. You don't know how to harness your limited time, energy and resources to move toward your enlightened self-interest."

"True."

"And your family gets shorted sometimes. Oh, who is your family? Debra, you mentioned. And two children who have grown and moved away. Tell me about them."

"Robert – he got tired of being called Bob Junior – and Rachel. Both doing well, with families of their own. We see each other when our schedules align, which isn't very often."

"For starters, identify your enlightened self-interest. You

know Debra is a major part of that, Robert and Rachel to a lesser extent at this stage in their own lives, plus they've got their own enlightened self-interests to pursue. But if you look at where you actually invest your limited time and energy, if you measure, do the numbers say Debra's a major part of your enlightened self-interest?"

"The numbers might indicate otherwise," Bob admits.

"But again, don't beat yourself up over it now. Fail forward. Failure is feedback. You can always learn from feedback. People who never fail are the ones hiding in the corner doing nothing at all because they're afraid to fail. Plus, they're lying. We all fail. So when you fail, so what? You failed. Own the problem and act on it. Move *toward* what you want, not *away* from what you don't want. We want you to focus on what you want, what's important to you, not on what you don't want."

"Yeah," Bob realizes. "Push and pull motivations. Like when people don't do something because they're afraid of the pain of getting fired, the pain of change, embarrassment, looking bad... sure, that stuff can be painful, so avoiding it is a motivation, but it'll only motivate you so far."

"That's right. You've got it. Push motivations are the ones that push you away from something bad."

"And pull motivations are much stronger because you're being pulled toward something. Your enlightened self-interest, your vision, something you can own and measure and be selfish about."

"That's right," says Rynd.

"I need to re-examine what's really in my best interest. My enlightened self-interest."

5

Chapter Five

Law #4: The Law of Ideas

Why do we have so many ideas?

How can we possibly act on them all?

"Great minds have purpose," says Rynd. "Others have wishes."

"I've heard that before," says Bob. "You're quoting someone."

Rynd nods. "Washington Irving."

"Some people might not even have a purpose."

"People can do a lot of things without one."

"They can run on auto-pilot, they can do what others do… It's about freedom, isn't it? That tunnel we talked about is restrictive. All you can do is go forward, or go back, or just stop. Either way, there's no freedom. No personal freedom, no financial freedom, no control over my own destiny, no meaning. Plus you can't even see what you're doing because you have tunnel vision. When I look back over my life, I want to know that it had some meaning in the bigger scheme of things. Wow, Debra knows that. Why don't I?"

"You do now."

"Why didn't I before?"

"There's no crime in being slow."

Bob laughs. "You're right. There's not. But you know, it's time to stop limiting myself. It's time to replace those defeating beliefs with the empowering attitudes and actions of successful people."

"Now or after you salvage the Eastern contract?"

Bob laughs again. "After. Hey, that's a big contract. It suits us so well."

"And you enjoyed telling Greg about it."

"I did! Wait. You're mentioning that now to teach me something, aren't you?"

Rynd doesn't answer.

"Aren't you?"

"No comment."

"Okay, fine, I'll figure it out."

"Unguarded thoughts," says Rynd. "Intuition. What feels right. Inklings that lead you into unexpected directions. Daydreams. Hobbies."

"If I watch those I might find my enlightened self-interest?"

Rynd nods. "You might."

"When I told Greg to reframe the requirements, that was fun. That was… it was teaching. Planning how to snatch victory from the jaws of defeat. Not micro-management, not grunt work, not sweating details, not putting out fires, not reacting to day-to-day problems. I felt that I was making real lasting progress there. That had meaning to me." Bob pauses. "To me."

Rynd nods. "You told Greg to reframe the proposal requirements."

"And now you're telling me to reframe my life."

"No, I'm not. *You're* telling you to reframe your life."

"Wow. Yes, I am. Reframe my life. Yes. Wow."

"You're starting to see it now."

"It's easier to see when I take myself out of the tunnel, isn't it? I can see that number I want, or thought I wanted. That million in annual gross sales. I can see what the numbers are now. Less than half that. I can see obstacles between where I am and where I think I want to be. But that's it. Not a lot of seeing going on there."

"Tunnel vision."

"Tunnel vision," Bob agrees. "Not a lot of new ideas. But if I get out of this metaphorical tunnel, and really look at everything…"

"You'll see too many new ideas."

"I will, won't I? I know so many people who are looking for that million dollar idea, but really, there are no new ideas."

"Plato said that."

"Was it his idea?"

Rynd laughs.

"They say *I need this idea,*" says Bob. "Or *I have this great idea* or *If I just came up with that right idea.* But there are so many ideas. Ideas about everything."

"Ideas about what kind of ideas."

"Rynd, sometimes I have an idea you want to be a comedian."

"That's not a bad idea."

"Oh, stop. But the thing is, we get more ideas than we can possibly act on. I've even caught myself doing it with my business. A lot, actually, which kind of contradicts what I was saying a minute ago. But if we actually set out to slow down and not be working every minute of every day and just think of some ideas, just brainstorm, then we get even more ideas. Far too many to act on. We just don't have the resources to do all that."

"True."

"So the question becomes how to decide which ideas… You've been waiting for me to say how to decide which ideas to act on for at least two minutes, haven't you? I could see it in your eyes."

Rynd nods. "Say it."

"We should examine our ideas and act on the ones that will take us closer to our enlightened self-interest."

"That's it."

"And this is only possible once we're clear on what our self-interest is in the first place."

"You've got it."

"If I like what I'm doing now, it's probably part of my enlightened self-interest. But if I don't still want to be doing that ten or twenty or forty years from now, then I should have a plan that includes me not still doing that ten or twenty or forty years from now. My new plan should take into account the fact that my enlightened self-interest has changed. But that's not going to happen if I'm not regularly considering new ideas and deciding which ones might better suit my enlightened self-interest later, which ones might better suit it now, which ones will probably never suit it at all."

Rynd nods. "A good idea that really suits somebody else's enlightened self-interest might not suit yours at all. And vice versa."

"I just thought of a good example of that. I know a guy who I think would be a fantastic writing coach or ghost writer. He doesn't do that kind of work now, but it's really not a far stretch for him to move into it. He could reinvent himself, define a whole new lifestyle, make a whole lot more money than he does now, work fewer hours and choose when to work them... Long story."

"Okay."

"But anyway, I gave him a whole lot of ideas on how to do this. Really good ideas. He agreed with me that they were good ideas, too. But then, well, he didn't do anything about it. He'd rather just take care of a faithful client base with consistent needs, And I sure appreciate being one of those faithful clients, of course, but I have wondered why he didn't act on those ideas."

"He couldn't bear to leave the light of your shining personality."

Bob laughs. "No, I think he decided that lifestyle, the one he'd have by acting on those ideas, wouldn't suit his enlightened self-interest. Not in those words, of course, but that's the general idea." Bob pauses. "Either that or he's really lazy."

Rynd laughs. "I can't comment because I've never met the guy."

"Change can be painful. Maybe avoiding that pain is keeping him from trying to change how he defines himself career-wise. Or maybe he just doesn't care about that at all. It's really not for me to say. I've got my own mess to straighten out."

"Calling it a mess might be exaggerating your condition."

"Probably. I've got my own enlightened self-interest to get clear on, then. But anyway, some people move away from pain or avoid pain, and some people go through pain to achieve their enlightened self-interest. Does that make sense?"

"Definitely."

"And if I'm doing something now that I don't want to be

doing a few years down the road, then I'm probably moving away from something and not toward something."

"Right."

"Not through something."

"Right."

"Not toward my enlightened self-interest."

"You've got it," says Rynd.

"When I take action to move away from pain and that pain stops, forward movement stops too. I've got a stimulus to get me started but no momentum to keep me going."

Rynd nods. "And how do you fix that?"

"Stay focused on my enlightened self-interest. If I do that, I'll embrace the actions necessary to achieve my selfishness by moving through the pain. And if I'm the type of person who needs pain to move forward, I need to know that and keep myself in some level of pain to ensure I don't stop moving."

"Don't get comfortable."

"Right. Don't get comfortable. Right now I'm a bit too mired in silly stress, though, not the kind of discomfort that would actually motivate me to do something about it, so that's not working either."

"Own that and change it."

"Yeah. I will. Keep thinking of new ideas, examine those, use my enlightened self-interest to decide what to do and when to do it and how to do it and why to do it. My enlightened self-interest is the key. It'll keep me motivated through the tough times, which let's face it is a problem for me right now." He pauses. "I do want that Eastern contract, though."

"Even though it just got harder to get?"

"Yep. I still want it. That'll give me the satisfaction of doing a difficult job and doing it well. I like that feeling. But some of the other work, somebody always has to do it, and it's educational and even fun, but after all this time I'd rather delegate that."

"It's not your purpose anymore."

"It's not my purpose anymore," Bob agrees. "Not my enlightened self-interest."

"Charles Darwin said that it isn't the strongest of species who survive, nor the most intelligent, but the one most responsive to change."

"The outside world changes and the inside world changes.

I need to change how I think. I need to create new skills, and I need to talk with people who have been there before me so they can show me the way. I can consider their ideas, measure those against my own enlightened self-interest. And that's the good kind of selfish, isn't it? The enlightened self-interest of knowing it, owning it, measuring it, sharing it…"

"I'm inspired."

Bob laughs. "I am going on a bit, aren't I?"

"That's fine."

"It is! It means I'm excited. That's a good feeling. A good intuition. Why didn't I see that before?"

"Maybe you should've wrecked the car before."

Bob groans and rolls his eyes. "Yeah. That's what I needed to do. No, wait… I think I'm having another epiphany here. I wrecked the car because I wasn't focused on what I needed to be, when I needed to be. Enlightened self-interest works better with focus."

"I agree with that."

"That's great, but really I don't care. What matters is that *I* agree with it."

"That's exactly right."

Chapter Six

Law #5: The Law of Focus

If it's not helping you get where you want to be, why are you doing it?

"It's hard to stay focused on important when you haven't realized what's really important," Bob continues.

"I can't argue with that."

"I knew a lady who was great at networking but whose efforts didn't lead to any new clients."

"That happens."

"It does, but she could be the poster girl for it. Her understanding of networking was to meet with everyone who wanted to meet with her."

"Again, that happens often enough."

"But almost every meeting ended with a request for her to open up her customer base to do joint marketing, and there was almost never a good reason for her to do this. She's an accountant, by the way. The odds of her customer base meshing with the customer bases of the people she networked with were pretty slim."

"I'll take your word for it. Business isn't my field."

"What is your field? I'd guess weightlifting."

Rynd laughs. "Close enough."

"Or secret agent, since you never tell me anything about yourself."

"No, definitely not secret agent man."

"Great song, by the way."

"Johnny Rivers or Devo?" Rynd asks.

"Either one. Whenever I asked my friend why she was meeting with a specific person, she answered, 'Isn't that what networking is all about?' I asked her what outcome she wanted. She didn't know. I asked her why she was meeting with him. Again, she didn't know. So I asked her, 'If you're meeting people without a clear objective of what you want from each meeting, how effective can you be?'"

"Not very," says Rynd.

"That's exactly what she realized. Meeting twenty people a week is an efficient way to create networking opportunities, but it's not an effective one."

"It's also probably exhausting."

"It is. That was sure measurable, twenty per week, but it's not focused. She needed a strategy. What do you want to accomplish from each meeting? Who is the best person to meet to achieve that? Is a next step defined? If not, why not? How much time, money, and energy do you have to invest to create this relationship, and is it worth it? Once she got clear on all that, on what she wanted from her networking, her business grew by 40% in less than a year."

"So you're better at focusing others than at focusing yourself," says Rynd with a laugh.

Bob grins. "So it would seem. Getting clear on my enlightened self-interest will keep my mind in order and attract what I need to make life more enjoyable. If I train myself to deliberately stay focused on my selfishness, I'll find that my thoughts and actions proceed in a more order-ly procession than ever before. That makes sense, doesn't it?"

"It does. Understanding your selfishness will make decisions easier and action clearer."

"But we can't stop there. It's too easy to abuse this concept and use it for unenlightened purposes. Using selfishness the way most people use it frames everything into an us-versus-them mindset. We are reframing what we mean when we say we're being selfish."

"How?"

"Intent matters. Focusing on what's important must always include my intent."

"Selfishness without the intent of being selfish," says Rynd.

"Right. We could call Mother Theresa, Gandhi, Henry Ford, and Martin Luther King prime examples of selfishness without the intent of being selfish. Mother Theresa devoted her whole life to working with the poor and indigent of Calcutta. Gandhi freed a nation through nonviolence. Henry Ford put a car in every garage."

Rynd deliberately looks at the wreckage. "We keep getting back to cars."

Bob chuckles. "Martin Luther King wanted to correct injustice. That's all enlightened self-interest. They accomplished great things through selfishness that otherwise would not have been possible. Through their enlightened self-interest – by focusing on that – they were selfless by accomplishing great things for others."

"Wow," says Rynd.

"Exactly," says Bob. "Wow." He pauses. "If the intent is malicious, the self-interest becomes selfish. If the intent is with good will, then it becomes enlightened self-interest. We're neither just in it for ourselves, nor just in it to help others. It's all gotta be in there or it's not enlightened, it's… it's tunnel vision."

"Which is not the focus we want."

"Not at all. We want nothing less than to focus on achieving greatness. And by greatness I mean taking action to achieve our enlightened self-interest, nothing more and nothing less. We often confuse notoriety with greatness. They are not the same. Being famous is not the same as doing great things."

"No matter what Twitter says."

"Twitter didn't say it. Some of its users did."

"Fair enough."

"To accomplish our greatness," Bob continues, "we have to understand that we have limitations. These limitations might be time, money, or other resources specific to our situation. Because it's impossible to accomplish our greatness unless we use our limited resources wisely, we must know what we want to achieve. We need to be intelligent in our use of these resources to accomplish our enlightened self-interest. Because we have so many people asking us to spend our hard-earned money, limited time, and precious resources, we must be very clear on what is important to us and be very selfish about using our resources to achieve this greatness."

"And that's the good kind of selfish."

"It is. With so many ideas to consider, from without and within, we need to know our enlightened self-interest so we can filter some out and focus on the rest. If I stay focused on my enlightened self-interest, obstacles will tend to disappear. Or at least if I do see them, they won't be as daunting as they might first appear. They'll become challenges to be overcome, new opportunities to be embraced, not obstacles that stop me. Taking inspired action to move forward requires me to take one step at a time, never losing sight of my end results, my enlightened self-interest."

"I'd certainly call that focus."

"So would I. And it's critical. I'm going to find it, own it, focus on it."

"How?"

"Step one, do a behavioral assessment that helps me understand my strengths and weaknesses. Two, compare those results to what I'm actually doing in my business and my life. Three, create a plan that allows me to spend more time doing what I'm good at and enjoy, and less time on things I don't enjoy and don't do well."

"Since you can't eliminate those things entirely."

"No, it's just not possible. Part of being realistic is to know that. But I'll outsource and delegate as much as I can. Step four, though, is to do the things that I don't like doing first, so I can move on to the fun stuff as quickly as possible. Step five, of course, is to just keep asking myself, is what I am doing taking me towards my enlightened self-interest."

"And if not, why are you doing it?"

"Exactly. If it has to be done, like I said, find a way to outsource it or delegate it." Bob pauses again. "I can't wait to get started."

"Doctor or customer?"

"Doctor, definitely. The customer can wait one more day. Staying healthy is definitely a better example of my enlightened self-interest."

"I once attended a funeral at which there was only one other person," says Rynd.

"And he was there looking for sales leads," quips Bob.

"No, I don't want that to be how I'm remembered. My enlightened self-interest can change over time, and many times it does change. I know people who have been doing the same work since college. That's not always wrong, but some people have a hard time understanding that the decisions they made in college were good decisions at the time, but as they grow, change and mature, what's important to them can change as well. That might be my problem – well, it might *have been* my problem, but now it's not."

"You're learning fast."

Bob nods. "Not bad for a guy with a possible head injury. When I left college, my primary focus was career, getting the right job, getting the money job, advancing in my chosen field. But then when Robert and Rachel were born, my focus changed. My needs changed. Then later, starting my own business was the main thing. Then growing it. And that was my focus, all good enlightened self-interest stuff even though I did it all by instinct rather than planning. And now it's just a rut, just a tunnel. It's time for me to focus on my enlightened self-interest, decide what really matters, and focus on that. I've been ignoring a major part of my enlightened self-interest, which is my need to grow."

"So what will you do?"

"Make one simple decision, take one action, take that one step that moves me to my greatness, however I define it. And I won't worry about how things are going to work out. My purpose is to take small steps, make small decisions. The universe will conspire to help me but the universe requires me to take action. Success is impossible without action. Success *is* action.

"And selfishness is a great idea which should be embraced and developed in my life. After I get clear on my selfishness, I can take inspired action to achieve my enlightened self-interest. The result of action is success, the outcomes I have worked so hard to achieve.

"And once I've got all that sorted out," Bob concludes, "keeping focus is really simple."

"It is?"

"It is."

"How so?"

"You know how."

"I do. But I want to hear you say it."

"Fine. I'll say it." Bob grins. "Is this going to take me closer to my enlightened self-interest? If not, why am I doing it?"

"That's focus."

"It is."

7

Chapter Seven

Law #6: The Law of

Self-Discipline

How do you keep yourself going in the face of failure?

"Habits are good too," says Rynd.

"They are," Bob agrees. "It's a lot of work to focus all your attention on everything you're doing and want to do, all the time. It's good to step back and consider all that, of course, and to do it often, but not 24/7."

"That'd be exhausting."

"Motion without achievement, actually. And that's exhausting. So habits are useful. Good habits. Successful habits. Habits that have been deliberately cultivated because they guide me to my enlightened self-interest."

"Those sound like good habits to have."

"I'm not going to succeed without self-discipline. And what is self-discipline? It's creating measurable, repeatable, and predictable success habits. First I get clear on what I want, and then I discipline myself to take the actions that will get me what I want, in a way that can be measured and repeated and predicted."

Rynd nods. "That'll work."

"But what if I fail?"

"Try again."

"Platitudes won't help me."

"It's true, Bob. If you fail, you just try again. That's a fact of life. I can't stop you from failing. We fail more than we succeed."

"Hmm. I suppose you're right."

"I am right."

Bob nods. "Okay. You're right. So… when we decide what we want, and we devise a plan to get us that thing we want, and it doesn't work – we fail, we don't get what we want, what happens? I guess we can give up, change what we want, say we never wanted it at all, but that's not honest. No, what we should do is see why it didn't work, why we didn't get what we wanted, and change something we're doing or assuming."

"Fail forward."

"Fail forward. That's a good way to put it. We learn something. We didn't get what we wanted, but we got information, and that's always useful to get. Knowledge. And we use that, and we try again to get what we want, but we do it in a different way. So if we're not just doing the same old thing again and again, it should be easier to not get dispirited when we fail, but to have the discipline to keep trying.

"Also, we shouldn't just go for the big score, the big grab, the *give me my million in annual gross sales* right away. That's not realistic, not achievable, not even logical really. You can't just go from zero to a million. You do it one contract at a time, one goal at a time, one step at a time. You break it down into measurable, actionable steps that have clearly defined completion dates."

"That's the difference between goals and dreams."

"It is," says Bob. "For example, a lot of people dream of writing a book, but most people never do it."

"I never have."

"Neither have I. But if I did, I wouldn't just sit down staring at a blank piece of paper or computer screen one day and boom, here comes a book. First I'd define my topic. Then I'd create my outline. Oh, and I'd do research of course. But from the outline, every day or week or whatever I decide, I'm going to fill in part of that outline. It's a roadmap, a schedule, a set of steps I can act on and measure. With the discipline to stick to that, I'll get that book written."

"I see."

"Oh, and it won't be done even then, because there's rewriting and editing and learning how to get published. But I'd turn all that into measurable and actionable steps too, after the steps that I'll think of as learning how to do all that stuff. That's focused, and it's disciplined. That's what works."

"No matter the goal."

"No matter the goal. Every goal can be broken down into smaller and smaller steps, until you've got a set of steps that you can achieve. Some steps take longer than others."

"It'll take you longer to drive to Arlington than it will to drive home from the office."

"Every single time. If I'm going to plan where I want to be five years from now, and I write that down and post it on the wall over my computer screen, and look at it every day, and call that my goal, I might get discouraged."

"You think?" Rynd asks with a grin.

"What'll happen to my self-discipline? Gone! So I break it down. Even when I was a student I had syllabuses and schedules for each semester, in a logical sequence, some classes building on what went before. Reading a bunch of textbooks might sound scary but reading a chapter a day sounds doable. And that way we don't get so overwhelmed that self-discipline is just impossible."

"Chunk it down."

"Chunk it down. It's easier to hold yourself accountable that way too. Did you write that book? Well, no, not today. Yes no, true false, ones and zeros, binary. That's not going to give us the discipline we need to get from here to there when getting from here to there requires a series of measurable, repeatable actions with predictable results."

"I see."

"So if I'm going to hold myself accountable for something, or give an assignment to one of my workers and hold him accountable for it, or ask someone else to hold me accountable for something –"

"Or pay him to hold you accountable."

"Right, or pay him to hold me accountable. Hey, that'd be an interesting job. Go around disciplining people all day and getting paid to do it."

"You're strange, Bob."

"Not all the time. But seriously, self-discipline is a whole lot easier that way. It makes more sense that way. And if I fail, so what? Learn, change the strategy, don't lose sight of my enlightened self-interest, don't get discouraged and just give up, actually be happy at how things are going even as the schedule changes. Gaining new information lets me make the schedule more realistic, which makes it easy to stay disciplined. I like this plan."

"So do I."

"Then you just have to persist. It's not a quick fix."

"We don't want it to be a quick fix. Those can be boring."

Chapter Eight

Law #7: The Law of Persistence

When whatever spurs you forward is removed, why should you keep moving?

"Persistence is the continuance of an effect after the cause is removed," says Bob. "We keep trying something until we get the results we want. That's what you mean by failing forward, isn't it?"

"It is. Like a rocket."

"What do you mean by that? No, wait, I know what you mean. A rocket is always adjusting to ensure it's on target. We need to do the same thing."

"That's right. Most people think a rocket goes from point A to point B without any adjustments, but that's not true. A rocket makes thousands of calculations, and thousands of adjustments, per second."

Bob nods. "It's fired, it goes through its calculations, it finds it's off course by three degrees, so it corrects. It finds that it has over-corrected and is now off two degrees in the other direction, so it makes another adjustment. It keeps doing this, failing forward, until it reaches its goal, which is its enlightened self-interest."

"You've got it," says Rynd.

"But how many times do you have to fail before you give up?" Bob asks.

"I hope you're not going to tell me that Thomas Edison tested ten thousand different ways of making a light bulb before he found the one that worked."

"No, I'm not," says Bob. "You already know that. Plus my office uses fluorescent lights, not filament bulbs. Needs change, and part of enlightened self-interest is knowing that. No, I have a different story to tell you."

"I'm all ears."

"It's good that you persist in listening, because that's what my story is about."

"Listening?"

"Persistence. I've done a lot of process redesign work in my career. Through this I learned the importance of persistence. I once worked with a large Midwestern bank. A team of us redesigned the accounts payable process. Our goal was to bring the payment processing time down from over 90 days to under 30 days."

"If a bank owed me money and I had to wait more than 90 days to get it, I wouldn't be pleased. At all."

"Exactly. Employees were not getting their expenses reimbursed in a timely manner and the bank was losing early payment discounts from vendors because they were missing deadlines, just to name two of the problems we identified."

"And a lot of people were annoyed."

"And a lot of people were annoyed," Bob agrees. "Productivity was measured by the number of invoices a clerk paid daily. When we started, each clerk was paying 75 invoices per day. After the process was redesigned and implemented, the same clerks were processing only 25 invoices per day."

"At first glance a failure."

"At first glance," Bob agrees with a smile. "You catch on fast, don't you? When they first transitioned to the new system, their production fell from 75 per day to 25 per day. If the company and the department had given up after we installed the new systems without giving the new actions a chance to fully develop, we would have been a failure."

"But I know they didn't give up because you're telling me this story."

"That's right, they didn't give up. They persisted, they learned the new system and mastered the new skills, until each clerk was paying between 275 and 325 invoices per day. One clerk actually processed 600 invoices in one day. Invoices were being paid in 24 hours, down from 90 days. Persistence pays off."

"But not if you persist in a cause that's doomed."

"This is true. If I set a goal of learning how to slam dunk a basketball, it wouldn't matter how many days I practiced, I'd never succeed. That form of persistence isn't so good."

"Being aware of that is a skill worth having."

"It is," Bob agrees, then grins. "Persistence is my cat demanding a meal."

Rynd laughs. "Focus, too. And success, I'll wager."

"It is. Cats always win."

"They own the Internet."

Bob's grin widens. "But whenever you learn something new, your performance suffers. Just watch a child learning to walk. He stands up, he stumbles, he sits down. Typically he'll smile because it was new and exciting. He'll repeatedly fail and that's okay. By failing he begins to understand what does not work. Eventually he puts everything together and takes the first step. But that's only the beginning. After that it's not long before he's running, skateboarding, bicycling.

At a young age he's passionate about learning. We should always be that passionate about learning."

"We should," Rynd agrees. "And I like that you mentioned bicycling, because another good example of persistence comes from that. Not the way I do it, for distance, but trick riding."

"My son used to do wheelies," Bob remembers. "Front tire off the ground wheelies, back tire off the ground wheelies, switching from wheel to wheel, sideways bounces, onto sidewalks, off sidewalks."

"And he came home bruised and bloodied a lot, didn't he?"

"All the time. Broken bones too, sometimes. Debra was so afraid he'd kill himself out there."

"Every time you see someone stunt ride, you're seeing persistence."

"Ah. Because he failed and fell and maybe even injured himself dozens of times before he mastered what looks so easy when you watch him now," says Bob. "But we don't want our businessmen coming home looking like failed gladiators."

"Even if they feel that way sometimes."

Bob grins. "Even if we feel that way sometimes. You know, entire websites have been built around the concept of doing a little bit every day. Books have been written about it. Whether you're trying to improve buzz marketing, lose weight, or quit smoking, they all take a change in habits and a daily commitment. And I'll only succeed if it is my decision to succeed."

"There are other examples, of course," says Rynd. "And Edison noted that many of life's failures are people who did not realize how close they were to success when they gave up."

"The list of so-called mistakes that turned out to be valuable and useful is legendary, isn't it?"

"Antibiotics," says Rynd. "Post-it notes, hard pretzels, vulcanized rubber, Ivory soap —"

"Ivory soap?"

Rynd nodded. "An operator forgot to turn off the mixer."

"I hadn't heard that one. Persistence paid for Milton Hershey, who failed several times in the candy making business before he came up with the Hershey bar."

"Walt Disney filed for bankruptcy twice."

"I haven't done that yet. I don't plan to, actually." Bob chuckles. "But like we agreed before, this isn't some quick fix solution we're creating here. Mistakes are essential to my success, as long as I learn from them and fail forward. If I set a good goal, one in my enlightened self-interest that I can chunk down and measure, and hold myself accountable, with persistence I will get there."

"You will. And your journey will be as fulfilling as the destination, much of the time, so it'll be easier to stay focused and disciplined and persistent."

"Not only will I hold myself accountable, but I'll get others in my life to hold me accountable. And it's good to finally be talking about others, isn't it?"

"It is," Rynd agrees. "No man is an island."

9

Chapter Nine

Law #8: The Law of People

How can you say it's selfish to help others?

"People are essential to our success," says Bob.

"They are. We need to understand that our success is 100% dependent on how well we lead, motivate, inspire, and influence others to take action."

"If others don't believe in what we're doing, in what motivates us, in our vision, do you know what happens? At best we get their compliance but not their commitment."

"Very true."

"Helping others is what it's all about. The most successful people are those who genuinely want to help others. It's easy to forget that in the rush, and it's always a big mistake."

"Do you mean friends and family, coworkers and colleagues, or customers and sales leads?" Rynd asks.

"All of them. But I'm going to start in the office, since that seems to be where I do most of my exploding lately."

"It's where you spend most of your time."

"Ha! That's true. People. Number one, don't try to change them. It'll just leave them frustrated and you exhausted. Focus on having others do what they're good at. There's a reason we often celebrate Joe Montana throwing to Jerry Rice but never Jerry Rice throwing to Joe Montana."

Rynd laughs. "This is true."

"Developing people's skills is always a worthwhile investment of your time. That can be helping your workers to move up in the organization. It can mean not helping them move up but helping them find a best fit within the organization instead. It's helping them develop skills that help them build on what's important to them as it pertains to organizational success. It's making them feel good about themselves, feeling confident and competent, and not just so they can help you someday. Darn it, it just feels good."

Rynd nods. "Something people might forget because it doesn't show up on a balance sheet."

"But it does. Those people do better work, and you do better work because you have them, and *that* shows up on the balance sheet. Offices full of sniping and petty squabbles never perform well. Certainly not long term, and probably not even short term. Plus, what about *my* vision and my selfishness? I don't want to be in a place like that."

"Me either."

"People can be unmotivated at work, but if you see them doing something after hours or on the weekends, they're almost always motivated about that."

"This is true."

"I want them to be that motivated in the office," says Bob. "I want *me* to be that motivated in the office. Being good with people is about getting them focused on their strengths and helping them build on what they already do well. It's taking ownership for providing opportunities for development, it's being persistent in making opportunities happen, it's teaching people why specific actions are important, and it's identifying and creating win/win situations in implementing my enlightened self-interest.

"People want to know that we trust them. Most of the time, when people buy into our vision and feel they can contribute, they will be loyal and productive. For trust to develop, especially in an organization, roles and responsibilities must be clearly defined. Many people thrive on knowing what they are allowed to do and what they are not allowed to do. When you put people in a position to succeed, the results can be powerful."

"So we want everybody to succeed," says Rynd, "not just for me to succeed while you don't."

"Of course. What happens when people are successful? Production increases, morale improves, and people want to stay in your organization or be around you because they know you will trust them to do the right thing."

"How do we do that?"

"Tell people exactly what we expect. Honesty, and more than that, candor."

"The Golden Rule."

"Always. Certainly. And also The Platinum Rule™," says Bob.

"I don't know that one."

"Treat others as they want to be treated. We all have different styles, preferences, skills, personality types. Some are more introspective, some more outgoing. Some visual, some aural, some kinesthetic. Don't assume everybody's like you. Hear them, know them, mesh with their styles and needs."

Rynd nods thoughtfully. "That makes sense. I like that."

"It applies to colleagues, to customers, and most importantly even friends and family. When Rachel – my daughter – was a little girl, she liked me to read her a story when she went to bed at night. So I did that. My son Robert, on the other hand, didn't want me to do that, so I didn't. It's how they wanted to be treated."

"What about when you were little?"

Bob returns Rynd's grin. "There's no way I can remember that far back. But I'm sure my parents treated me the way I wanted to be treated, whatever it was. The Platinum Rule."

"What if I don't want you selling me your product?"

"You're just being naughty now."

"Who? Me?"

Bob grins. "The Platinum Rule says I shouldn't sell it to you. But guess what? Nobody likes being sold to. Nobody. But what they do want is for us to teach them how to buy. If I've got a service that will genuinely help you, it would be remiss of me not to tell you. And no, I'm not just splitting hairs. I mean this."

"I can see that."

"Persuasion does not mean manipulation. Sales is not reaching into a bag of tricks. It's honesty. Selling is helping a person do what they actually want or need to do. We sell spouses on doing what we want."

"Like marrying you?"

"Absolutely. We sell children on being respectful, doing well in school, staying away from drugs. Children sell parents on getting that toy. Older ones sell parents on letting them stay out past curfew. Teachers sell students on learning."

"I have to admit that I never thought of it that way."

"And you're not just saying that to make me feel good."

"Would you want me to?"

Bob laughs. "In this case, no. So, Platinum Rule, you're telling me the unvarnished truth because that's what I want to hear."

"I always do that anyway. I'm not very good at reading people."

Bob laughs again, then lays a hand on Rynd's shoulder. "Learn, my friend. Learn."

The two men pause for a moment, lost in their own thoughts. Bob is thinking about how quickly he's formed a deep bond with a man he's only just met. That happens sometimes, and it's always a pleasant surprise.

Bob is also wondering where that ambulance is. He

doesn't feel the need, but it knows it's best to be safe and let an expert decide. He's also wondering where the tow truck is, but that's just idle curiosity rather than genuine concern.

"If I'm associating with people who don't support my enlightened self-interest," he says, "I should consider associating with other people instead. I need to read books that bring me closer to what I want. Listen to books that bring me closer. Use visualization techniques to bring me closer. Come to think of it, that's how I improved my golf game."

"How?"

"Advice from experts, books, videos, watching other golfers, watching Debra golf, getting advice from Debra, giving advice to Debra, watching videos of myself."

"I've never done that."

"You should. It's great."

"Can I borrow Debra?"

"No." Bob grins hugely. "Oh, and another way to improve a golf game is better equipment. In the case of my business, in the case of my whole life, my brain and my attitude are my equipment. I can improve them. If I keep my enlightened self-interest in my mind, and keep thinking about it, and visualize it like that perfect golf swing, or like pushing through the pain to jog farther than I ever have before, it has to happen."

"It's hard to take action, especially inspired action, if you don't care deeply about something," says Rynd.

"It is. And now I'm starting to realize what I care deeply about. I want to teach and inspire and motivate people. I want to be known and respected for my honesty and my common sense. I want people to come away from whatever it is thinking *that Bob sure helped me* because I did. I want to control what I do and when I do it. I want more time to do the things I love doing that aren't in the office. And of course I want more time to be with Debra who I love and my children who will make time for me if I let them. And I want to share what I've learned, to give something back.

"As we change our attitudes and beliefs," he continues, "we will scare others in our lives. As we change our actions we'll scare some of them. Some will change with us; others will leave. It is not easy but the rewards will be exactly what we want, especially when we get clear on what's important to us."

"And those others influence us as well," says Rynd. "If we continue to associate with people who reinforce our negative belief systems, how can we expect to get past those negative belief systems and implement the changes we need to make?"

"It just won't happen," says Bob.

"That's why we need to surround ourselves with people who will support us in achieving our goals."

"Changing is hard enough without letting others stop us," says Bob. "Ownership is the first step in learning to think differently."

"It is."

"Knowing the role people play in making this happen is an important second step. So, we need to choose the people in our lives carefully. We must take everything and everyone into consideration as we choose the path to our goals."

Rynd nods. "Our actions are connected to everything and everyone."

"They are. And again, helping other people brings me genuine satisfaction. They benefit from my helpfulness, which in turn inspires them to accept both my personal and my corporate vision. This is a prime example of the win/win philosophy, which is my enlightened self-interest, good selfishness rather than bad selfishness. Bad selfishness, narrow selfishness, just leads to stress and frustration and bad feelings all around. It's not healthy or selfish at all."

"It's just tunnel vision."

Bob nods. "And very misguided. But enlightened self-interest, helping others for the sheer joy of it, is always good."

"So when we first met," says Rynd, "you gave yourself permission to be selfish. Now you're giving yourself permission to help others."

"Yes!"

10

Chapter Ten

Law #9: The Law of Action

Why bother creating a new definition of success unless you act on it?

"Since our goal is to give me permission to succeed," says Bob, "we should probably decide what success is."

"That makes sense."

"If I ask other people what success means to them, I'll probably hear a lot of different answers."

"You probably will."

"They'll talk about being happy, making more money and achieving financial freedom, having more family time, better relationships, less stress."

"I think they'll mention more money a lot."

"They will. But what do they mean by that? Does more money mean having enough to eat out when you want to? Does it mean being able to pay for your children's college? Does it mean having a great retirement, a new home, a nicer car, or better clothes?"

"Back to the car," says Rynd.

"Any car would be nicer than that, wouldn't it?"

Rynd nods. "If you can't define something you can't achieve it."

"Exactly. So I have to determine what success means to me. If I say it's being happy, what does being happy mean? What is financial freedom? How much family time is enough family time? What makes a relationship better? Like you said, if I can't define it I can't achieve it."

"I see a pattern here."

"So do I," says Bob. "People confuse the outcomes of success with being successful. So first we need a new definition of success, and then we need to act on it."

"Success is to take action," says Rynd. "All these definitions we've discussed – money, financial freedom, family time, better relationships, lower stress – are the results of taking action."

"That's it," Bob agrees. "Success is action. To be a success, I have to act. Inaction can only be corrected by action. Or as my father used to drawl, 'Do something even if it's wrong.' When in doubt, I need to do something. Clarity comes from action. Act, learn from the action, and then act again based on what I've learned. Use what I learn every day. Knowledge without action is useless.

"I can have all the skills and knowledge necessary to achieve my desired outcomes, but if I don't act on that knowledge and use those skills, they're useless. Action is the cornerstone of success."

"Even unsuccessful action."

"That's right. Most action, if unsuccessful, can be corrected by taking different action. Inaction can never be corrected, except by action."

"And personal improvement."

Bob nods. "That's crucial. How much time and money do people spend on personal improvement, learning new skills and making themselves indispensable? I don't know, but they'd better spend *some* time on it."

"True."

"There are many ways to acquire this knowledge. Books, tapes, audio programs, online learning websites, courses, seminars, etc."

"And making mistakes."

"And making mistakes," Bob agrees. "When mistakes happen, as they will, like we said before, that's okay too. There are no mistakes. Failure is feedback. Fail forward, and grow from it."

"Grow and change."

"Right."

"Failure is feedback. That could be a bumper sticker."

"Or at least a tweet," says Bob. "As you grow it's not uncommon to change what you do and how you do it. The very act of growing can refine and clarify your decisions. People sometimes assume that the decisions they made in college cannot be changed. Not only can they be changed, but they should be changed if they no longer work for you. You have changed, you are more mature, and you have a better understanding of what is important to you. Use this knowledge, and don't fret if you have some difficulty."

"It's a process not a destination."

"Right. If you know what life you want, use the process as a refresher to reaffirm your past decisions and to refocus on the life you would like to live. Revisit the process often. As you grow and change it is likely your goals and outcomes will change with you."

"Mine certainly have."

"Mine too. Not realizing that has been a mistake, but one I'm going to learn from."

"Not bad for a guy with a possible head injury."

Bob grins. "Not bad at all. When deciding what to do

next, don't run *from* something, run *to* something. Know what your strengths are, explore what you want to do, try things out, and learn."

"It sounds simple, doesn't it?"

"That's because it is," says Bob. "Sometimes it really is."

11

Chapter Eleven

Bob's Journey Continues

Birds.

Bob hears birds.

Bob doesn't know how long it's been since he last noticed hearing the birds. He listens a moment longer. Leaning back, eyes closed, he feels the breeze and enjoys the smells of nature.

"I've spent all this time thinking that the way to quit working so hard is to gross a million a year. But there's another way to stop working so hard, and that's to just stop. Simple as that. I'll stop."

Bob chuckles. "Specifically, I'm going to move from constantly growing my business to letting someone else take over. Maybe Greg. Or Ella. Or both. They'd make a nice couple, actually. I'm going to focus on consulting. I can help more people that way, and I can enjoy life more that way.

"I'm going to stop staying busy just for the sake of being busy or to keep the boredom at bay. Motion isn't always action. I'm going to stay busy doing what matters to me – busy but not too busy – even if that's just giving myself permission to relax, golf, jog, meditate, go camping, read, whatever.

"What do you think?"

Bob waits. Rynd doesn't reply. Bob opens his eyes.

"Hmm. Where'd you go?"

Bob pauses, then laughs quietly.

"I know he was here. I didn't make that up."

Bob hears the siren and knows that the ambulance will arrive before the tow truck. He goes to his car and sees that the driver's side door is open. The seat belt and the airbag have both been slashed by a sharp knife, which makes his job easier. He grabs a pen and paper so he can write down what he's learned.

-o0o-

Bob looks up as a tall young man enters his office.

"Happy Father's Day," says Robert. "Well, two days late, but still."

Bob quickly rises and moves around his desk to greet his son. Robert reaches out a hand, but Bob surprises him by enfolding him in a warm hug.

"Oh," says Robert, smiling. "It's good to see you too, Dad."

"Let's go."

"Now as in right now? No waiting five minutes while you make one last call, finish one last sales forecast, bark out one last batch of orders to your people?"

"I'm ready right now. Woof woof."

Robert laughs as the two men leave the office and fall into step beside each other.

"Before we go," says Bob, "Ella wants to show you something."

"Cool. Isn't her office up that way?"

"Not anymore."

"Okay. Oh, I saw your new car. It looks a whole lot like your old one."

"Sometimes I get set in my ways."

"That's news to me, Dad. Oh, Mom said you two are finally taking a vacation next month."

Bob grins. "Surprised?"

"Maybe," Robert admits.

"You're an IT guy. You know that running a computer at 100% capacity all the time will eventually lead to a system failure. Why would you expect a human being to be any different?"

"I wouldn't."

"And you thought I would?"

"Maybe." Robert is distracted from his train of thought by an unfamiliar woman pushing a vacuum cleaner in the carpeted hallway. They let her pass, and then Robert says, "New hire?"

Bob shakes his head. "Cleaning service. This isn't a one-man shop with a few jack-of-all-trade helpers anymore. Outsourcing makes more sense. Let my people do what they're best at, and spare them some aggravation."

"Wow."

"Including payroll. Especially payroll."

"Wow. So Mom says you're going to St John. Are you going there for the kayaking, the cave diving, the kiteboarding, or the horseback riding?"

Bob laughs. "You know I'm too old for that."

"Forty-five isn't old."

"True. But I was too old for what you're talking about when I was twenty-five. No, we're just going to relax and enjoy."

"Sounds great. But aren't you worried?"

"About what?"

"Your sales will plummet."

"Who are you imitating in that silly voice?"

"Monty Python. Crunchy Frog."

"You're too young to memorize Monty Python."

"You're never too young to memorize Monty Python."

"Even so, I believe our sales can survive without me. Especially since I've got a new company president."

"You what?"

"I promoted Greg. I'm still CEO, of course, but he's running things for the most part. You know he's got the skills."

"That's true. I'm just kind of surprised."

"So was he. Even though he did win the Eastern contract without me."

"You're different, Dad. Happier. More relaxed. What's different?"

I had a long talk with Rynd six months ago and haven't seen him since.

"I'm learning to delegate more," Bob says. "Especially to

Greg. The promotion really suits him. I can kick back, relax, coach, mentor."

Robert grins. "So the company's paying you for your mind and not your body now."

Bob laughs. "Pretty much."

The plaque on the office door reads *Ella Pierson, Purchasing Manager.* Inside, Ella meets Robert's gaze with a smile and holds up a manicured finger. She's on the phone. Robert and Bob wait.

"I'll see you then," she says, then hangs up the phone and moves around the desk to give Robert a hug.

"Success suits you," he says.

"So does this," she says, showing him the engagement ring on her hand.

"Wow. Nice. Who's the lucky guy?"

Ella laughs. "Greg. Of course." She turns to Bob. "You guys heading out?"

"Yeah. So was that another applicant on the phone?"

"It was."

Bob turns to Robert. "Ella's trying to find someone who can replace her as my assistant. Once she narrows it down

I'll interview whoever and make a decision."

"We've got a temp out there right now," Ella adds.

"So how's it going?" asks Robert.

"Badly," Ella laughs, then turns to Bob. "I'll have two or three people ready when you get back from St John."

"Sounds good to me." He turns to Robert. "You ready?"

"Let's do it. Oh, wait, how's Richard? The last member of the old gang. Is he here now?"

"No, he coaches his son's soccer team on Tuesdays."

"In an Armani?"

The three of them laugh.

"He still doing inside sales?" Robert asks.

"No. We realized that we were mistaking his ability to do it so well with him actually being satisfied with it. He's handling Receivables and Payables right now."

"So he's still staying in the office but dressing better than anyone going out on the road."

"That's his enlightened self-interest in action."

"His what?"

Bob grins. "It seems to *suit* him."

Robert groans. Ella rolls her eyes.

As Bob and Robert leave the office, Bob thinks that how he learned about his enlightened self-interest really isn't important. What matters is that he knows about it now, and that he is going to act on it. Always.

12

Chapter Twelve

The Nine Laws of

Enlightened Self-Interest

The Law of Enlightened Self-Interest: It's okay to be selfish. In fact, it's good to be selfish, provided that it's the right kind of selfish.

The Law of Total Ownership: Take total ownership for where you are in your business and your life. If you don't own it, you can't change it.

The Law of Measurable Results: Measure all results and implement what works so others can take the same actions. We tend to notice what we can measure and ignore what we can't measure.

The Law of Ideas: The problem is never a shortage of ideas. The problem is that we have too many ideas. By evaluating them against our enlightened self-interest, we will know which ideas to keep and which ideas to eliminate.

The Law of Focus: Stay focused on what is important. Without focus we just stumble into the future.

The Law of Self-Discipline: Be disciplined on doing what works, no matter how difficult it gets. If it isn't working, there's no reason to keep doing it.

The Law of Persistence: Be persistent. When you implement something new, your performance will suffer until you have mastered this new behavior.

The Law of People: Always strive to help others. This will bring you satisfaction and give your life meaning. Surround yourself with people and resources who can help you with inspired ideas that take you deeper into your enlightened self-interest. Whenever someone or something can help you achieve your goals, there is no reason not to use them. Be equally helpful when others want your help to achieve their enlightened self-interest.

The Law of Action: Success is action and failure is feedback. Take action to achieve your enlightened self-interest, and learn from both the actions that work and the actions that fail.

About The Authors

Ron Finklestein: Speaker, Business Consultant, International Author, Business Growth Facilitator

"Small Business Success Expert" "Entrepreneur." "Passionate" "Leader." "Motivator." "Get Results." "Team Builder." This is how business leaders and clients describe Ron.

After a successful consulting career, Ron has spent the past 10 years building his business and helping entrepreneurs and business owners build their businesses. Ron is called The Small Business Success Expert by his clients because of his passion for their success and his knowledge of business. Ron has experience in working with businesses across a wide range of industries (Manufacturing, Banking, Government, Healthcare, Outsourced Services, Technology Industries, and Insurance) and on every aspect of a business, from information technology to marketing, leadership to sales, allowing him to offer practical and proven ideas and strategies to improve any business.

Ron knows and understands that all successful people exhibit nine behaviors and he has built products to help implement these behaviors in businesses of all sizes. Because of the depth of breadth of Ron's experience, he can quickly and decisively see and identify business and personal challenges, identify innovative solutions and create opportunities out of most any problem.

Ron has owned his business since 2002 and enjoys helping grow and improve small businesses:

Twenty-five years of Fortune 1000 consulting experience

International author of Management and Leadership book called *The Platinum Rule for Small Business Mastery* with Dr. Tony Alessandra and Scott Zimmerman, *49 Marketing Secrets (That Work) to Grow Sales, Nine Principles for Inspired Action: A New & Targeted Perspective. And Celebrating Success! 14 Ways to Create a Successful Company.*

Owner of RPF GROUP INC, which provided business coaching and consulting services to business owners and entrepreneurs to help them build a better business (www.businessgrowthexperience.com.)

Ron has an established reputation for building strong relationships and using those relationships to help others enhance their own personal and professional success. Ron is a frequent speaker and presenter on various business topics including *Building Businesses*, *Leadership*, *The Platinum Rule®*, *Attitudes and Behaviors of Success*, *Sales and Marketing*, *Entrepreneurship*, *Business Strategies* and *Business Mastery*. Ron is involved with numerous business, non-profit organizations and initiatives as part of his personal commitment to personal and professional growth and the growth of his clients.

Currently, Ron resides in Fairlawn, Ohio. He spends his time consulting, coaching small business owners to greater success, writing and speaking about how to implement success strategies in business.

Over the years Ron has spoken to or for business groups, chambers of commerce, community groups, associations, in-house training programs, continuing education programs, seminars, lunch and learns, workshops, etc. Participants and attendees have described Ron as "energizing", "enthusiastic", "fun", "engaging", "motivational", "thoughtful", "informative", "inspiring", "effective", and "motivating." If you are interested in learning how Ron can help you in your business or to have Ron speak to your business, team, organization, association or group, contact him at

http://www.ronfinklestein.com
ron@ronfinklestein.com

Michael LaRocca was a purchasing manager and technical editor for an Engineering/R&D firm for eight years before moving to China in 1999 and creating MichaelEdits.com. Prior to that he was a computer programmer, military electronics specialist, hog farmer and repo man.

Michael spent six years teaching English in China, five years as a medical lecturer in Thailand, and one year in Vietnam continuing to grow his business. In those 12 years, he traveled everywhere by bicycle, so returning to North Carolina included remembering how to drive.

Michael returned to North Carolina in 2011 with his lovely Australian wife, who he married in October 2000, and the Calico cat they adopted from the Hong Kong SPCA in September 2000. He likes to tell people, "I bring home the best souvenirs."

Michael has also written 12 published books, mostly novels. His non-fiction works include Teach Yourself Creative Writing and Who Moved My Rice? He can be reached at

MichaelEdits.com
MichaelWrites.com

CPSIA information can be obtained
at www.ICGtesting.com
Printed in the USA
FFOW02n1947200913
1854FF

9 781628 650174